Let's Sing Songbook

Volume 2

D1411851

Produced by K12 Inc.

Art Director: Steve Godwin

Illustrator: Margaret Georgiann

ISBN: 1-931728-47-X

Printed by Worzalla, Stevens Point, WI, USA, April 2013, Lot 042013

Table of Contents

How To Teach A Song

Songs

Poems and Chants

How To Teach A Song: A Choice Of Methods

In the K12 Music program, you will help your student learn to sing many songs. When a lesson calls for the student to learn a new song, you have a choice of teaching methods.

Use Method A if you are not comfortable with singing or confident about your own ability to sing. Use Method B if you feel confident of your ability to sing in tune for the student. These teaching methods are designed to present the information in small chunks, rather than all at once. They will help the student learn songs quickly and thoroughly.

A: The Song Sheet Method

Step 1: Learn the Words
Read each line of words out loud and ask the student to say the words after you. Begin with one line at a time. Increase the number of lines each time you repeat the song until the student can say the words to the whole song.

Step 2: Sing the Melody

Listen to the CD selection. Repeat the selection and say the words with the student in the rhythm of the melody. You and the student sing along with the CD. When the student is comfortable singing the song, proceed to the activity.

B: The Singing Method

Step 1: Prepare

Before you teach the lesson, learn to sing the song using the CD and lesson song sheet. Sing along with the CD until you feel comfortable with the song at the pitch level on the CD. Songs on the CD are recorded in a pitch range appropriate for the healthy development of a child's voice.

Step 2: Learn the Melody

Listen to the CD selection with the student. Sing the melody of the first phrase using a wordless syllable, such as la, instead of the words. Point to the student to indicate that he or she should echo or sing back the phrase you've just sung. Continue until you have sung all the phrases of the song. If the student sings a phrase incorrectly, simply repeat it until he or she sings it correctly.

Sing the song again, but this time, sing two phrases at a time. Point to the student when it is his or her turn to sing.

Step 3: Add the Words
Sing the song with the words, one phrase at a time, and ask the student to echo you. Continue until you have sung all the phrases with the words.

Sing the song again but increase to two phrases at a time. When the student is comfortable singing the song, proceed to the activity.

Revisit

A song introduced in one lesson will often be repeated in later lessons. When you encounter the same song in a later lesson, repeat either of the above procedures as needed. Encourage the student to sing the song once on his or her own. This will help the student develop the confidence needed to sing alone. Be sure to praise the student's efforts.

Songs

All Night, All Day

All night, all day,

Angels watching over me, my Lord.

All night, all day,

Angels watching over me.

Now I lay me down to sleep,

Angels watching over me, my Lord.

Pray the Lord my soul to keep,

Angels watching over me.

All night, all day,

Angels watching over me, my Lord.

All night, all day,

Angels watching over me.

If I die before I wake,

Angels watching over me, my Lord.

Pray the Lord my soul to take,

Angels watching over me.

The Birch Tree

See the lovely birch in the meadow,
Curly leaves all dance when the winds blow.
Liu-li, liu-li, the winds blow,
Liu-li, liu, in the meadow.

When I play my new balalaika,
I will sing of you, my little birch tree.
Liu-li, liu-li, the winds blow,
Liu-li, liu, in the meadow.

Bounce High, Bounce Low

Bounce high, bounce low,
Bounce the ball to Shiloh.

Bow, Wow, Wow

Bow, wow, wow,
Whose dog art thou?
Little Tommy Tucker's dog,
Bow, wow, wow.

Brother Martin

Brother Martin, Brother Martin.

Wake, awake, wake, awake.

Bells are ringing.

Bells are ringing.

Ding, dong, ding.

Ding, dong, ding.

Button You Must Wander

Button you must wander, wander, wander.

Button you must wander everywhere.

Bright eyes will find you.

Sharp eyes will find you.

Button you must wander everywhere.

Bye, Bye Baby

Bye, bye baby, baby bye,

My little baby, baby bye.

C'est la Nuit

C'est la nuit,

Plus de bruit.

Ecoutez làbas minuit,

Qui sonne, qui sonne.

Cock Robin

Who killed Cock Robin? Who killed Cock Robin?

"I," said the sparrow, "with my little bow and arrow,

It was I, oh, it was I."

Come Back Home My Little Chicks

Call: Come back home my little chicks.

Response: We won't come.

Call: Why not?

Response: We're afraid.

Call: Of what?

Response: Of the wolf.

Call: Where's he hiding?

Response: In the woods.

Call: What's he doing?

Response: Washing.

Call: What's he drying his face on?

Response: On the kitty-cat's tail!

The Deaf Woman's Courtship

Old woman, old woman,
Are you fond of smoking?
Speak a little louder, sir,
I'm very hard of hearing.

Old woman, old woman,
Are you fond of carding?
Speak a little louder, sir,
I'm rather hard of hearing.

Old woman, old woman,
Don't you want me to court you?
Speak a little louder, sir,
I just began to hear you.

Old woman, old woman,
Don't you want to marry me?
Lord have mercy on my soul,
I think that now I hear you.

Doggie, Doggie

Doggie, doggie, where's your bone?

Someone stole it from your home.

Who stole my bone?

Fais Do-do

Go to sleep, my sweet little brother,

Go to sleep, and you'll get a treat.

Go to sleep, my sweet little brother,

Go to sleep, and you'll get a treat.

Oh, mother's upstairs,

Some cookies she'll bake.

And father's downstairs,

Sweet chocolate to make.

Go to sleep, my sweet little brother,

Go to sleep, and you'll get a treat.

Go to sleep, my sweet little brother,

Go to sleep, and you'll get a treat.

Frère Jacques

Frère Jacques, Frère Jacques,

Dormez-vous? Dormez-vous?

Sonnez les matines, sonnez les matines,

Din, din, don! Din, din, don!

Fudge, Fudge

Fudge, fudge, call the judge,

Mamma's gonna have a baby.

Not a girl, not a boy,

Just a plain old baby.

Wrap the diaper up in tissue,

Throw it down the elevator.

First floor, stop!

Second floor, stop!

Third floor, you better not stop 'cause H-O-T spells hot!

Grandma Grunts

Grandma Grunts said a curious thing,
"Boys may whistle but girls must sing!"
That is what I heard her say!
'Twas no longer than yesterday.

Grandma Grunts said a curious thing,
"Girls may whistle but boys must sing!"
That is what I heard her say!
'Twas no longer than yesterday.

Great Big Dog

Great big dog come a-runnin' down the river,

Shook his tail and jarred the meadow.

Go 'way old dog, go 'way old dog,

You shan't have my baby.

Mother loves you, Father loves you,

Everybody loves baby.

Mother loves you, Father loves you,

Everybody loves baby.

Great Big House in New Orleans

Great big house in New Orleans,
Forty stories high.
Every room that I've been in,
Filled with pumpkin pie.

Went down to the old mill stream,
To fetch a pail of water.
Put one arm around my wife,
The other 'round my daughter.

Fare thee well, my darling girl,
Fare thee well, my daughter.
Fare thee well, my darling girl,
With the golden slippers on her.

Green, Green, the Crabapple Tree

Green, green, the crabapple tree,

Where the grass grows so deep.

Miss Emma, Miss Emma,

Your true lover is dead.

He wrote you a letter,

To turn back your head.

(Repeat using different names.)

Head and Shoulders

Head and shoulders, baby, one, two, three.
Head and shoulders, baby, one, two, three.
Head and shoulders, head and shoulders,
Head and shoulders, baby, one, two, three.

Knee and ankle, baby, one, two, three.
Knee and ankle, baby, one, two, three.
Knee and ankle, knee and ankle,
Knee and ankle, baby, one, two, three.

Throw the ball, baby, one, two, three.
Throw the ball, baby, one, two, three.
Throw the ball, throw the ball,
Throw the ball, baby, one, two, three.

Milk the cow, baby, one, two, three.
Milk the cow, baby, one, two, three.
Milk the cow, milk the cow,
Milk the cow, baby, one, two, three.

I ain't been to Frisco and I ain't been to school.

I ain't been to college but I ain't no fool.

To the front to the back, to the side, side, side.

To the front to the back, to the side, side, side.

To the side, side, side, to the side, side, side.

Hey, Ho, Anybody Home

Hey, ho, anybody home?

Meat nor drink nor money have I none.

Still I will be very merry.

Hey, ho, anybody home?

I Lost the Closet Key

I've lost the closet key in that lady's garden.

I've lost the closet key in that lady's garden.

Help me find the closet key in that lady's garden.

Help me find the closet key in that lady's garden.

I've found the closet key in that lady's garden.

I've found the closet key in that lady's garden.

I Lost the Farmer's Dairy Key

I lost the farmer's dairy key,

I'm in this lady's garden.

Do, do, let me out,

I'm in this lady's garden.

Jim Along Josie

Hey, jim along, jim along Josie,

Hey, jim along, jim along Jo.

Hey, jim along, jim along Josie,

Hey, jim along, jim along Jo.

Walk, jim along, jim along Josie,

Walk, jim along, jim along Jo.

Walk, jim along, jim along Josie,

Walk, jim along, jim along Jo.

Hop, jim along, jim along Josie,

Hop, jim along, jim along Jo.

Hop, jim along, jim along Josie,

Hop, jim along, jim along Jo.

Johnny Cuckoo

Here come one Johnny Cuckoo, cuckoo, cuckoo,
Here come one Johnny Cuckoo,
On a cold and stormy night.

What did you come for, come for, come for,
What did you come for,
On a cold and stormy night?

I come for many a soldier, soldier, soldier,
I come for many a soldier,
On a cold and stormy night.

You look too ragged and dirty, dirty, dirty,
You look too ragged and dirty,
On a cold and stormy night.

I'm just as clean as you are, you are, you are,
I'm just as clean as you are,
On a cold and stormy night.

Jubilee

It's all out on the old railroad, it's all out on the sea,
All out on the old railroad, far as I can see.

Chorus:
Swing and turn, jubilee!
Live and learn, jubilee!

Hardest work I ever done, working on the farm,
Easiest work I ever done, swing my true love's arm.

Chorus

Coffee grows on a white oak tree, sugar runs in brandy,
Girls as sweet as a lump of gold, boys as sweet as candy.

Chorus

Some will come on Saturday night, some will come on Sunday,
And if you give them half a chance, they'll be back on Monday.

Chorus

If I had a needle and a thread, fine as I could sew,
I'd sew my true love to my side, and down this creek I'd go.

Chorus

In some lady's fine brick house, in some lady's garden,
Let me out or I'll break out, fare ye well, my darlin'.

Chorus

If I had no house at all, I'd be found a-crawlin',
Up and down this rocky road, lookin' for my darlin'.

Chorus

All I want is a big, fat horse, corn to feed him on,
Pretty little boy to stay at home, and feed it when I'm gone.

Chorus

The Juniper Tree

Oh, sister Phoebe, how merry were we,
The night we sat under the juniper tree.
The juniper tree, hi-o, hi-o,
The juniper tree, hi-o.

Hat on your head will keep your head warm,
And one or two kisses will do you no harm.
Will do you no harm, I know, I know,
Will do you no harm, I know.

Go choose a partner, so choose you a one,
Go choose you the fairest that ever you can.
Now rise up you, gal, and go, and go,
Now rise up you, gal, and go.

King's Land

I'm on the king's land,
The king is not at home.
He's gone to Boston,
To buy his wife a comb.

Kookaburra

Kookaburra sits in the old gum tree,
Merry, merry king of the bush is he.
Laugh, Kookaburra, laugh, Kookaburra,
Gay your life must be.

Kookaburra sits in the old gum tree,
Eating all the gumdrops he can see.
Stop, Kookaburra! Stop, Kookaburra!
Leave some there for me!

Kumbaya

Kumbaya, my Lord, kumbaya.
Kumbaya, my Lord, kumbaya.
Kumbaya, my Lord, kumbaya.
Oh, Lord, kumbaya.

Someone's crying, Lord, kumbaya.
Someone's crying, Lord, kumbaya.
Someone's crying, Lord, kumbaya.
Oh, Lord, kumbaya.

Someone's laughing, Lord, kumbaya.
Someone's laughing, Lord, kumbaya.
Someone's laughing, Lord, kumbaya.
Oh, Lord, kumbaya.

Someone's singing, Lord, kumbaya.
Someone's singing, Lord, kumbaya.
Someone's singing, Lord, kumbaya.
Oh, Lord, kumbaya.

Someone's praying, Lord, kumbaya.
Someone's praying, Lord, kumbaya.
Someone's praying, Lord, kumbaya.
Oh, Lord, kumbaya.

Kumbaya my Lord, kumbaya.
Kumbaya my Lord, kumbaya.
Kumbaya my Lord, kumbaya.
Oh, Lord, kumbaya.

Lady Come Down

Lady come down and see,
The cat is in the plum tree.

Lemonade

Call: Here I come!

Response: Where from?

Call: New York.

Response: What's your trade?

Call: Lemonade.

Response: Give us some, don't be afraid.

(Repeat using different cities.)

Little Sally Water

Little Sally Water, sitting in a saucer,

Rise, Sally, rise, Sally, wipe away your tears, Sally.

Turn to the east, Sally, turn to the west, Sally,

Turn to the one that you love best.

Long-Legged Sailor

Have you ever, ever, ever in your long-legged life,

Seen a long-legged sailor with a long-legged wife?

No, I never, never, never in my long-legged life,

Seen a long-legged sailor with a long-legged wife.

Have you ever, ever, ever in your short-legged life,

Seen a short-legged sailor with a short-legged wife?

No, I never, never, never in my short-legged life,

Seen a short-legged sailor with a short-legged wife.

Have you ever, ever, ever in your cross-legged life,

Seen a cross-legged sailor with a cross-legged wife?

No, I never, never, never in my cross-legged life,

Seen a cross-legged sailor with a cross-legged wife.

Have you ever, ever, ever in your bow-legged life,

Seen a bow-legged sailor with a bow-legged wife?

No, I never, never, never in my bow-legged life,

Seen a bow-legged sailor with a bow-legged wife.

Have you ever, ever, ever in your one-legged life,

Seen a one-legged sailor with a one-legged wife?

No, I never, never, never in my one-legged life,

Seen a one-legged sailor with a one-legged wife.

Have you ever, ever, ever in your no-legged life,

Seen a no-legged sailor with a no-legged wife?

No, I never, never, never in my no-legged life,

Seen a no-legged sailor with a no-legged wife.

Mamalama

Mamalama cumalama cuma-la-pizza.

Mamalama cumalama cuma-la-pizza.

Oh, no, no, no, no la pizza.

Oh, no, no, no, no la pizza.

Anie manie dixapane ooh-op-a lumba lene.

Ochee cotchee avawatchee X-Y-Z!

Anie manie dixapane ooh-op-a lumba lene.

Ochee cotchee avawatchee X-Y-Z!

Mister Rabbit

Mister Rabbit, Mister Rabbit, your ear's mighty long.

"Yes, my Lord, they're put on wrong."

Ev'ry little soul must shine, shine,

Ev'ry little soul must shine, shine, shine.

Mister Rabbit, Mister Rabbit, your foot's mighty red.

"Yes, my Lord, I'm almost dead."

Ev'ry little soul must shine, shine,

Ev'ry little soul must shine, shine, shine.

Mister Rabbit, Mister Rabbit, your coat's mighty grey.

"Yes, my Lord, 'twas made that way."

Ev'ry little soul must shine, shine,

Ev'ry little soul must shine, shine, shine.

Mister Rabbit, Mister Rabbit, your tail's mighty white.

"Yes, my Lord, I'm gettin' out o' sight."

Ev'ry little soul must shine, shine,

Ev'ry little soul must shine, shine, shine.

The Mocking Bird

Hush, little Minnie, and don't say a word,

Papa's going to buy you a mocking bird.

It can whistle and it can sing,

And it can do most anything.

My Landlord

My landlord rang the front doorbell,

I let it ring for a long, long spell.

I went to the window, I peeped out the blind,

And I asked that man what was on his mind.

He said, "Money, honey, ooo-wee!

Money, honey, ooo-wee!

If you wanna get along with me,

If you wanna get along with me."

Old Brass Wagon

Circle to the left, old brass wagon.

Circle to the left, old brass wagon.

Circle to the left, old brass wagon.

You're the one, my darlin'!

Circle to the right, old brass wagon.

Circle to the right, old brass wagon.

Circle to the right, old brass wagon.

You're the one, my darlin'!

Swing, oh, swing, old brass wagon.

Swing, oh, swing, old brass wagon.

Swing, oh, swing, old brass wagon.

You're the one, my darlin'!

Promenade around, old brass wagon.

Promenade around, old brass wagon.

Promenade around, old brass wagon.

You're the one, my darlin'!

Old Joe Clark

Chorus:

'Round and 'round, old Joe Clark,

'Round and 'round I say.

'Round and 'round, old Joe Clark,

I ain't got long to stay.

Old Joe Clark, he had a house,

Sixteen stories high.

Every story in that house,

Was full of chicken pie.

Chorus

Old Joe Clark, he had a dog,

Blind as he could be.

Chased a red bug 'round a stump,

And a coon up a hollow tree.

Chorus

I went down to old Joe's house,

Never been there before.

He slept on the feather bed,

And I slept on the floor.

Chorus

If you see that girl of mine,

Tell her if you can,

Before she goes to make up bread,

To wash those dirty hands.

Chorus

When I was a little boy,

I used to play in ashes.

Now I am a great big boy,

Wearing Dad's mustaches.

Old Roger

Old Roger is dead and he lies in his grave,
Lies in his grave, lies in his grave.
Old Roger is dead and he lies in his grave,
Ai-ya, a-yo, a-yay!

They planted an apple tree over his head,
Over his head, over his head.
They planted an apple tree over his head,
Ai-ya, a-yo, a-yay!

The apples grew ripe and they all fell down,
All fell down, all fell down.
The apples grew ripe and they all fell down,
Ai-ya, a-yo, a-yay!

There came an old woman a-pickin' them up,
Pickin' them up, pickin' them up.
There came an old woman a-pickin' them up,
Ai-ya, a-yo, a-yay!

Old Roger got up and he gave her a thump,
Gave her a thump, gave her a thump.
Old Roger got up and he gave her a thump,
Ai-ya, a-yo, a-yay!

Which made the old woman go hippety-hop,
Hippety-hop, hippety-hop.
Which made the old woman go hippety-hop,
Ai-ya, a-yo, a-yay!

The Paw Paw Patch

Where, oh, where is pretty little Susie?

Where, oh, where is pretty little Susie?

Where, oh, where is pretty little Susie?

Way down yonder in the paw paw patch.

Come on, boys, let's go find her.

Come on, boys, let's go find her.

Come on, boys, let's go find her.

Way down yonder in the paw paw patch.

Pickin' up paw paws, put 'em in her pockets.

Pickin' up paw paws, put 'em in her pockets.

Pickin' up paw paws, put 'em in her pockets.

Way down yonder in the paw paw patch.

Pizza, Pizza

Judith has a boyfriend,

Pizza, pizza, daddy-o.

How do you know it?

Pizza, pizza, daddy-o.

'Cause she told me,

Pizza, pizza, daddy-o.

Let's rope it!

Rope it, rope it, daddy-o.

Let's throw it!

Throw it, throw it, daddy-o.

Let's end it!

(Repeat using different names.)

Que Llueva

Que llueva, que llueva,

La rana está en la cueva.

Los pajaritos cantan,

La luna se levanta.

Que sí, que no!

Le canta el labrador.

Rock, Rock

Rock, rock, how you wander,

From one hand into the other.

Is it fair, is it fair,

To see poor Anna sitting there?

(Repeat using different names.)

Rocky Mountain

Rocky mountain, rocky mountain, rocky mountain high,

When you're on that rocky mountain,

hang your head and cry.

Do, do, do, do, do remember me,

Do, do, do, do, do remember me.

'Round and 'Round

'Round and 'round we must go,

Boom, makaleli, chee, chee boom.

Down Miss Patty you must go,

Boom, makaleli, chee, chee boom.

(Repeat using different names.)

'Round the Mountain

Here we go 'round the mountain, two by two.

Here we go 'round the mountain, two by two.

Here we go 'round the mountain, two by two.

Rise, sugar, rise!

Show your pretty motion, two by two.

Show your pretty motion, two by two.

Show your pretty motion, two by two.

Rise, sugar, rise!

Run, Children, Run

Run, children, run, the patter-roller catch you,

Run, children, run, it's almost day.

Run, children, run, the patter-roller catch you,

Run, children, run, it's almost day.

This child ran, this child flew,

This child lost his Sunday shoe.

Run, children, run, the patter-roller catch you,

Run, children, run, it's almost day.

Sailing on the Ocean

Sailing on the ocean, the tide rolls high,

Sailing on the ocean, the tide rolls high,

Sailing on the ocean, the tide rolls high,

You can get a pretty girl by and by.

Got me a pretty girl, stay all day,

Got me a pretty girl, stay all day,

Got me a pretty girl, stay all day,

We don't care what the others say.

Eight in the boat and it won't go 'round.

Eight in the boat and it won't go 'round.

Eight in the boat and it won't go 'round.

You can have the pretty girl you just found.

Scotland's Burning

Scotland's burning, Scotland's burning.

Look out, look out!

Fire, fire, fire, fire!

Pour on water, pour on water.

Shake That Little Foot

Old Aunt Dinah went to town,

Riding a billy goat, leading a hound.

Shake that little foot, Dinah-O,

Shake that little foot, Dinah-O.

Hound dog barked and billy goat jumped,

Set Aunt Dinah straddle of a stump.

Shake that little foot, Dinah-O,

Shake that little foot, Dinah-O.

Old Aunt Dinah sick in bed,

Sent for the doctor, the doctor said.

Shake that little foot, Dinah-O,

Shake that little foot, Dinah-O.

Get up Dinah, you ain't sick,

All you need is a hickory stick.

Shake that little foot, Dinah-O,

Shake that little foot, Dinah-O.

Shake Them 'Simmons Down

Shake that tree, do-oh, do-oh,

Shake that tree, do-oh, do-oh,

Shake that tree, do-oh, do-oh,

Shake them 'simmons down.

Circle right, do-oh, do-oh,

Circle right, do-oh, do-oh,

Circle right, do-oh, do-oh,

Shake them 'simmons down.

Circle left, do-oh, do-oh,

Circle left, do-oh, do-oh,

Circle left, do-oh, do-oh,

Shake them 'simmons down.

'Round your partner, do-oh, do-oh,

'Round your partner, do-oh, do-oh,

'Round your partner, do-oh, do-oh,

Shake them 'simmons down.

Promenade all, do-oh, do-oh,

Promenade all, do-oh, do-oh,

Promenade all, do-oh, do-oh,

Shake them 'simmons down.

Skating Away

There were two couples a-skating away,

A-skating away, a-skating away.

There were two couples a-skating away,

So early in the morning.

The ice was thin and they all fell in,

They all fell in, they all fell in.

The ice was thin and they all fell in,

So early in the morning.

The old swing out and the new swing in,

The new swing in, the new swing in.

The old swing out and the new swing in,

So early in the morning.

Skin and Bones

There was an old woman all skin and bones,

Oo-oo-oo-oooo.

One night she thought she'd take a walk,

Oo-oo-oo-oooo.

She walked down by the old graveyard,

Oo-oo-oo-oooo.

She saw the bones a-lyin' around,

Oo-oo-oo-oooo.

She went to the closet to get a broom,

Oo-oo-oo-oooo.

She opened the door and . . . BOO!

Sorida

Sorida, Sorida, -ri-da, -ri-da.

Sorida, Sorida, -ri-da, -ri-da.

Da, da, da. Da, da, da, -ri-da, -ri-da.

Da, da, da. Da, da, da, -ri-da, -ri-da.

Stoopin' on the Window

Stoopin' on the window, wind the ball.

Stoopin' on the window, wind the ball.

Stoopin' on the window, wind the ball.

Stoopin' on the window, wind the ball.

Let's wind the ball, again, again, again!

Let's wind the ball, again, again, again!

Unwind the ball, again, again, again!

Unwind the ball, again, again, again!

That's a Mighty Pretty Motion

That's a mighty pretty motion, dee, di, dee,

That's a mighty pretty motion, dee, di, dee,

That's a mighty pretty motion, dee, di, dee,

Rise, sugar, rise!

That's a mighty poor motion, dee, di, dee,

That's a mighty poor motion, dee, di, dee,

That's a mighty poor motion, dee, di, dee,

Rise, sugar, rise!

Tideo

Pass one window, tideo.

Pass two windows, tideo.

Pass three windows, tideo.

Jingle at the windows, tideo.

Tideo, tideo, jingle at the windows, tideo.

Tideo, tideo, jingle at the windows, tideo.

Tisket, a Tasket

A tisket, a tasket,

A green and yellow basket.

I wrote a letter to my love,

And on the way I dropped it.

I dropped it, I dropped it,

And on the way I dropped it.

Tue, Tue

Tue, tue, barima tue, tue.

Tue, tue, barima tue, tue.

Abo fro ba amma dowa, dowa, tue, tue.

Abo fro ba amma dowa, dowa, tue, tue.

Barima tue, tue.

Barima tue, tue.

Turn the Glasses Over

I've been to Haarlem, I've been to Dover,

I've traveled this wide world all over.

Over, over, three times over,

Drink what you have to drink and turn the glasses over.

Sailing east, sailing west,

Sailing over the ocean.

Better watch out when the boat begins to rock,

Or you'll lose your girl in the ocean.

Wall Flowers

Wall flowers, wall flowers, growing up so high,

May had the measles and never, never died.

Call to Jeanie Butler's house,

She has no relations.

She may tick and tack and turn her back,

And wave to the congregation.

(Repeat using different names.)

We Like Pizza

We like pizza,

We like pizza, one turn around now.

(Repeat using different foods.)

Who's That Tapping at the Window

Who's that tapping at the window?

Who's that knocking at the door?

Mommy tapping at the window.

Daddy knocking at the door.

Who's That Yonder?

Who's that yonder, dressed in red?
Must be the children that Moses led!
Who's that yonder, dressed in white?
Must be the children of the Israelite!

Who's that yonder, dressed in pink?
Must be Solomon, tryin' to think!
Who's that yonder, dressed in green?
Must be 'Zekiel in his flyin' machine!

Who's that yonder, dressed in black?
Must be the hypocrites a-turnin' back!
Who's that yonder, dressed in blue?
Must be the children that are comin' through!

Wishy Washy

Oh, we are two sailors lately come from sea,
And if you want another one, come along with me.
Oh, wishy washy wishy washy wishy washy wee,
And if you want another one, come along with me.

Poems
and Chants

Queen, Queen Caroline

Queen, Queen Caroline,

Washed her hair in turpentine,

Turpentine to make it shine,

Queen, Queen Caroline.